Patrick Henry

by
Stuart A. Kallen

Visit us at
www.abdopub.com

Published by ABDO Publishing Company, 4940 Viking Drive, Edina, MN 55435. Copyright ©2001 by Abdo Consulting Group, Inc. International copyrights reserved in all countries. No part of this book may be reproduced in any form without written permission from the publisher.

Printed in the United States.

Graphic design: John Hamilton
Cover Design: Maclean Tuminelly

Cover photo: Corbis
Interior photos and illustrations:
    Corbis: p. 5, 6, 9, 11, 12, 15, 19, 25, 33, 35, 38, 41, 45, 46, 49, 51, 53, 55, 57
    North Wind Picture Archives: p. 17, 21, 29, 31, 43, 59

Library of Congress Cataloging-in-Publication Data

Kallen, Stuart A., 1955-
    Patrick Henry / Stuart Kallen.
        p. cm. — (The founding fathers)
    Includes index.
    ISBN 1-57765-012-3
    1. Henry, Patrick, 1736-1799—Juvenile literature.
2. Legislators—United States—Biography—Juvenile literature. 3. Virginia—Politics and government—1775-1783—Juvenile literature. 4. United States—Politics and government—1775-1783—Juvenile literature. 5. United States—Politics and government—1783-1789—Juvenile literature. 6. United States—Continental Congress—Biography—Juvenile literature. I. Title.

E302.6.H5 K35 2001
973.3'092—dc21
[B]
                                                    98-004688

Contents

Introduction

IN RICHMOND, VIRGINIA, 1775, the state's leaders gathered together in St. John's Church. Thirty-nine-year-old Patrick Henry was among them. Henry was arguing for an American revolution. He wanted to be free from British rule. To fight the British, Henry wanted to raise a statewide militia. Other leaders opposed him. They were afraid to anger England, the world's most powerful country.

Henry spoke his case quietly and respectfully to those who disagreed. He said, "We have been trying for the last 10 years. Shall we beg England yet again to listen to us? We have done that many times. We have sent petitions. We have asked humbly. We have done everything that could be done to avert the storm which is now coming on."

Facing page: A portrait of Patrick Henry.

"They tell us we are weak," Henry continued. "But when shall we be stronger? Will it be the next week, or the next year? Will it be when we are totally disarmed, and when a British guard shall be stationed at every house? The war is inevitable—and let it come. I repeat... let it come."

Then came the words that are still famous to this day: "Is life so dear, or peace so sweet, as to be purchased at the price of chains and slavery? I know not what course others may take; but as for me... give me liberty or give me death!" When he said "death," he waved an iron letter opener and pretended to stab himself. The audience was stunned into silence. Soon America and England would be at war.

Facing page: Patrick Henry giving his famous speech in which he said, "Give me liberty, or give me death."

The Virginia Plantations

JOHN HENRY was a well-educated man. He had gone to college in Scotland. When he came to America he married Sarah Syme—a very educated woman. Together, the Henrys lived on a Virginia plantation called Studley.

The Henrys' son, Patrick, was born on May 29, 1736. Eight daughters and another son were born after Patrick. The busy Henry home also included John Syme, Jr., a son from Sarah's first marriage.

Virginia and the other 12 colonies were ruled by Great Britain. Large tobacco farms dotted the colony of Virginia. Wealthy planters tried to copy the lifestyle of rich English people. But the Henrys lived a simpler lifestyle. They treasured books, which were rare and costly at that time.

There were no public schools in Virginia. Teachers were not available for backwoods children. Patrick went to a tiny country school off and on until he was 10. Then John decided he would teach the child himself. Patrick learned some Greek, Latin, and math from his father.

Slaves working on a tobacco plantation.

Storekeeper to Plantation Farmer

ALTHOUGH HIS FAMILY treasured learning and studying, Patrick did not. He would rather hunt, fish, and prowl the forests. When young Patrick broke his collarbone (while he and his brother were trying to break a wild colt!), he taught himself to play violin and flute as he was healing. Patrick was a good listener. He would listen when his father talked about books, religion, and politics.

When Patrick was 14, his father decided that there was no reason to waste money sending him to college. Instead, he sent Patrick to work in a country store to learn a trade. When Patrick was 16, John Henry bought him a store to run. The store never made much money, and finally failed by the time Patrick was 19. But young Patrick Henry didn't care. He was about to get married.

An old-fashioned country store.

A battle from the French and Indian War.

In 1754, Patrick married 16-year-old Sarah Shelton. Sarah's father gave the couple a 300-acre (121-hectare) plantation called Pine Slash. He also gave the couple six slaves to run the farm. Patrick worked next to his black slaves hoeing, picking worms off tobacco, and feeding the animals. The Henrys had one child when a fire destroyed their farm. Patrick sold the slaves to raise money to open another store.

In 1759, a bad tobacco crop ruined many farmers. The Henrys' store was not doing well since no one had any money to buy anything. At the same time Great Britain was fighting France in Pennsylvania and the Ohio Valley. Many of Patrick's friends went off to fight. They wanted to keep the American colonies out of French hands. Everyone's taxes went up because the British needed to pay for the French and Indian War.

Music, Dancing, and Pleasure

THE FRENCH AND INDIAN WAR set people to talking about politics. American and British soldiers were fighting the French together, but there were problems. The English looked down their noses at Americans. And the English would not let Americans sell their crops in any country except England. Americans complained bitterly. They wanted to sell their goods in France, Spain, and elsewhere.

Patrick Henry's second store went out of business in 1759, but he didn't seem to mind. During the Christmas season, Henry entertained at parties with his flute and fiddle.

At one party Henry met a teenager named Thomas Jefferson. Jefferson was a serious scholar on his way to college in Williamsburg, Virginia. The teen, who would one day be president, didn't

A fiddler at a barn dance.

think much of the fun-loving Patrick Henry. Jefferson wrote: "His manners had something of coarseness in them. His passion was music, dancing, and pleasure."

Still, Henry needed to make a living to support his growing family. He wasn't much of a storekeeper, so what could he do? He could talk. And what professions called for a good "talker?" Ministers, teachers, and lawyers all needed this skill. However, to be a teacher or a minister required years of study. So Patrick Henry decided to become a lawyer.

The Virginia Lawyer

AFTER THE HENRYS' STORE failed, the family moved into a room in the Hanover Tavern. Sarah's father owned the inn. The Hanover County courthouse was across the street from the tavern. Six of the 12 justices on the court were Patrick's relatives. Patrick often sat in the courtroom listening to interesting cases.

In April 1760, Patrick rode his horse into Williamsburg, Virginia. Four of the colony's finest lawyers agreed to test Patrick so he could get a law license. Patrick had read only two law books and studied for less than six months. Lawyer John Randolph quizzed Patrick for several hours. Patrick did not know cases, but he could argue his side with great force.

Randolph was not impressed with Patrick's legal knowledge. But he was impressed with his intelligence. After Patrick promised to study more, Randolph signed a license for him to practice law.

Facing page: Colonial Williamsburg, Virginia.

Sparkling Blue Eyes

HENRY STUDIED his law books and worked on several cases for his relatives. Meanwhile, the couple lived at the tavern where Henry served customers and played his fiddle.

As his law practice grew, Henry spent time arguing cases in other counties. Sometimes he would ride his horse 100 miles (161 km) to a distant court. Other times he would walk 15 miles (24 km) to work.

Henry won most of his cases. He had a way of getting a jury to agree with him. He studied jury members by watching their faces and hands. He started out slowly to get their attention. Once he got going he would fix his eyes on the jury. Henry was known for the startling gleam in his sky-blue eyes. By winning so many cases, Henry began to make good money.

An actor portraying Patrick Henry.

In his first three years at law practice, Henry argued 1,185 cases. That equaled about one case a day spread over six Virginia counties. By 1764, Henry was doing so well that he was able to lend money to his father. By 1767, he was able to lend money to Sarah's father.

Henry began buying large tracts of land. The family moved often. They needed bigger and bigger houses because their family kept growing. The Henrys had three sons and three daughters. By the time their last child was born, Patrick Henry was well known throughout Virginia.

The Two Penny Law

A CASE THAT WOULD HELP make Patrick Henry famous began December 1, 1763. The case known as the "Parson's Cause," started when Reverend James Maury tried to force tax collectors of Louisa County to give him more pay. The reverend's case was based on an old law that Henry strongly opposed.

Under this law, every Virginia taxpayer had to pay its Anglican minister (parson) in tobacco every year. In years when tobacco sold for good prices, ministers earned a lot of money. When tobacco prices fell, ministers earned less. One year the price of tobacco went so high that ministers earned a small fortune—about 400 English pounds, more than two times what Henry earned in a year as a successful lawyer.

Facing page: a hand-colored engraving of Patrick Henry.

Virginia's lawmaking body, the House of Burgesses, thought this was too much money to pay ministers. They passed a law saying parishes should pay in money instead of tobacco. They set the rate at two pennies per 100 pounds of tobacco harvested. This law became known as the "Two Penny Law."

This law was very popular because it saved taxpayers a lot of money. It was especially popular with people who went to other churches but were still forced to pay Anglican ministers. But the ministers appealed to England to change the law. The English king struck down Virginia's Two Penny Law. Once the law was repealed, ministers went to court to get their money.

Things did not look good for people who opposed the ministers. A lower court had already ruled that the ministers should get the tobacco. Since the case looked doomed, the Louisa County lawyer quit. Patrick Henry stepped in at the last moment. The judge was his father, John Henry. This was the first case Patrick Henry had argued in open court.

Facing page: England's King George III struck down Virginia's Two Penny Law.

The court was packed with 20 other ministers. They smiled as Patrick stumbled over his words. John Henry was embarrassed for his son. Suddenly, Patrick's head snapped up and his shoulders went back. His blue eyes flashed at the jury. His deep voice rose and fell. The jury laughed when Patrick made a few jokes. Then they gasped at his shocking statements. Patrick's voice blazed with scorn and anger. No one in the room had ever heard such a speech. Tears ran down John Henry's face.

Patrick Henry spoke of the role of government and the role of the church. He attacked the idea of a church paid for by the taxpayers. He criticized England for striking down a law made in Virginia. He reminded jurors that the ministers had upset a law passed by Virginia's elected representatives. He said the job of ministers was to make people obey laws. But they refused to obey the Two Penny Law.

Patrick Henry said if the ministers did not obey the law, "instead of useful members of the state, they ought to be considered enemies of the community... [that] has no further need of the ministry, and may justly strip them of their jobs." Patrick Henry went on to call the ministers "greedy harpies" who did not "worry about feeding and clothing the poor." He said they only "worried about their own pay."

Patrick Henry attacked the idea of a church paid for by taxpayers.

*Artist George Cook's painting of Patrick Henry
arguing the Parson's Cause case.*

Patrick Henry went on. He said the English king had no right to set aside laws passed by Virginia's elected leaders. He said a king who sets aside laws was not the father of his people but "a tyrant who forfeits all rights to his subject's obedience."

The Reverend Maury's lawyer jumped to his feet. He said Patrick Henry had "spoken treason." The 20 other ministers in the courtroom began yelling and arguing. Soon they stomped out of the courtroom. Most people in the crowd were laughing. Patrick Henry appealed to the jury. He said the jury alone could decide how much to pay a minister. They might even decide a minister was only worth one farthing (less than a penny).

In less than five minutes the jury gave its verdict—one farthing for Reverend Maury. The amount was an insult to the minister. The crowd cheered. People lifted Patrick Henry on their shoulders and paraded him around the courtroom.

Patrick Henry had attacked both the English church and the English government. The Parson's Cause was one of the first cases that called for keeping church and state separate. It was also the first step in Patrick Henry's career as a revolutionary.

Rumblings of Revolution

I N 1765, PATRICK HENRY was elected to Virginia's House of Burgesses—the lower house of the Virginia Assembly. The plainly dressed, 29-year-old Henry was ignored by the wealthy delegates as he went to his first Assembly session.

The delegates were complaining about a new tax that had been handed down from the English law-making body called Parliament. England needed to raise money after winning the French and Indian War. Since the war was fought to protect the colonies, Parliament thought that the Americans would be glad to pay taxes. They were wrong.

The new tax was called the Stamp Act of 1765. It was a tax on nearly every piece of paper in the colonies including legal documents, newspapers, and even playing cards. No one dared to speak out publicly. The tax was to go into effect in five months, on the first of November.

Patrick Henry arguing before the Virginia Assembly.

Henry was the newest and youngest member of the House. He was expected to sit quietly and learn from the others. But on that day in May, Henry rose and moved that the House take on the Stamp Act. He had written some resolves. Thomas Jefferson, who was there, said Henry spoke out with "torrents of sublime oratory."

Henry said that "the General Assembly of this colony have the sole right and power to lay taxes on the people of this colony. Any attempt to take away that power has a tendency to destroy British as well as American freedom."

The representatives rose from their seats. The new fellow had just said that Virginians did not have to obey laws passed by Parliament. Some threatened to harm Henry. Others insulted him. Henry argued back. Shouts rang through the room, "Treason! Treason!" Henry shouted back, "If this be treason, make the most of it!"

After heated arguments, the House approved Henry's resolve to end the Stamp Act. Henry was the first to speak out against it, but soon others followed.

One of the few notes Henry left behind concerned the Stamp Act speech. He wrote: "The alarm spread throughout America with astonishing quickness... The great point of resistance to British taxation was... established in the colonies. This brought on the war which finally separated the two countries and gave independence to ours."

After one year of protests, British Parliament repealed the Stamp Act. However, their troubles were just beginning.

Examples of Stamp Act stamps.

Family Tragedy

PATRICK HENRY was a busy man for the next 10 years. He was elected again and again to the House of Burgesses. But his law practice kept him so busy that he barely had time to attend the Assembly.

Well-known and successful, Henry bought a 16-room mansion on 1,000 acres (400 hectares) called Scotchtown in 1771. Little did he know of the personal tragedy that lay in his future.

After the birth of their sixth child, Sarah Henry's mind began to slip as her health failed. By 1772, Sarah Henry had gone completely insane. She had to be tied down in a special dress or she would hurt herself and others. Sarah had to be spoon-fed meals and watched over at all times. It was a sad and difficult time.

Scotchtown, the mansion Patrick Henry and his family moved to in 1771.

Defending Rights

ALTHOUGH THE HENRYS had slaves, Patrick was against slavery. In 1773, he wrote that Christians should not support the slave trade because it was "against humanity, against the Bible, and destroys liberty." Although he wrote against slavery, Henry still owned 67 slaves by the time he died.

Henry also felt strongly that people should have freedom of religion. He spent some of his time defending Baptist or Presbyterian ministers who had been jailed for practicing their religion. Others had to pay heavy fines for preaching their beliefs.

A new royal governor, Lord Dunsmore, was appointed in Virginia in 1773. Lord Dunsmore closed the House of Burgesses several times so the

The work-weathered hands of a former slave from Greene County, Georgia.

lawmakers would not stir up more trouble for England. This forced the lawmakers to meet secretly in a nearby tavern.

In Massachusetts, Samuel Adams had started a group called the Committees of Correspondence. Committees were set up in villages and towns to update people with the latest news and politics. Virginia set up its own Committees of Correspondence. Patrick Henry was the leader.

Tea Taxes and Boycotts

PARLIAMENT REPEALED the Stamp Act, but they soon passed a group of new taxes. The Townsend Acts levied taxes on glass, paint, paper, and tea brought in from Britain.

The tax on tea was only a few pennies, but it enraged Americans. Every time they had a cup of tea, people were reminded that the British controlled them. People were urged to boycott (stop buying) British tea.

The Committees of Correspondence kept close track of the tea boycott. On December 16, 1773, people in Boston, dressed as Indians, dumped chests of tea into Boston Harbor. The event was known as the Boston Tea Party. A few months later, the British decided to punish the people of Boston by closing the port there.

Facing page: the Boston Tea Party.

The House of Burgesses wanted to show that they supported the people of Boston. Lord Dunsmore dismissed them once again.

Assembly members met again at the tavern. They urged Virginians to support the boycott against English goods. The Committees of Correspondence called for a general congress of colony leaders. Messengers went to other colonies to spread the news.

In August 1774, Patrick Henry, George Washington, and six others were elected to represent Virginia at the First Continental Congress. The congress would meet in September in Philadelphia. These men were risking their lives. England could declare them traitors and hang them.

Facing page: Carpenters' Hall, in Philadelphia, Pennsylvania, scene of the First Continental Congress in 1774.

Not a Virginian, But an American

THE FIRST Continental Congress opened session on September 5, 1774, in Carpenters' Hall in Philadelphia, Pennsylvania. Since there had never been such a meeting, there were no rules to follow. Virginia was the biggest colony with the most people. Would it have the most votes? Henry didn't think so. He pointed out that British soldiers were camped out on Boston Common. The British navy was anchored in many colonial ports. And the British had closed all the courts because of unrest.

Henry urged the colonies to work together. He said, "The distinctions between Virginians, Pennsylvanians, New Yorkers, and New Englanders are no more. I am not a Virginian, but an American." This was a bold new idea to many delegates. The Continental Congress agreed that Americans must fight to rid themselves of British taxation.

At the end of October, Henry returned to Virginia. Sarah was very sick. In 1775, she died. This personal tragedy did not stop Patrick Henry. When he returned to Hanover, he called up volunteers for a local militia. The men trained with old rifles and no uniforms. They were about to take on the most powerful country in the world.

Patrick Henry speaking before the First Continental Congress in Philadelphia, Pennsylvania, in 1774.

Liberty or Death

LORD DUNSMORE was ready to arrest Henry and other Virginia leaders. When they met in Richmond in early 1775, Henry gave a speech that would become famous. Henry urged Virginia to raise a statewide militia. He reminded those who opposed him that Americans had been begging England for freedom for 10 years. He said: "The war is inevitable—and let it come. I repeat... let it come. I know not what course others may take; but as for me... give me liberty or give me death!"

Thomas Jefferson stepped forward to take a vote. The delegates agreed with Henry, who was appointed to a committee to make plans. Henry and six others were elected to go back to Philadelphia for the Second Continental Congress. Before Henry left for Philadelphia he saw militiamen training with the slogan "Liberty or Death!" stitched onto their shirts.

Facing page: Patrick Henry shouting "Give me liberty, or give me death!"

Gunpowder Perils

WITH MILITIAS training and revolution in the air, the British were nervous. Orders came from British generals to seize all gunpowder stored in the colonies. This would disarm the militias. When the British soldiers, nicknamed "redcoats," tried to take the gunpowder in Massachusetts, the first battles of the Revolutionary War were fought in Lexington and Concord.

In Virginia, Lord Dunsmore used British marines to secretly seize the militia's gunpowder in the middle of the night. It was stored in Williamsburg. The people of Williamsburg discovered the theft the next morning.

Facing page: actors portraying English troops (redcoats) prepare for a recreation of the Battle of Lexington.

The Governor's Mansion at Williamsburg, which Patrick Henry's militia troops threatened to attack.

On May 2, 1775, Henry and several hundred volunteers from Hanover began a march on the Governor's Mansion. They demanded that Dunsmore return their powder.

The governor panicked. He passed out rifles to his slaves. Dunsmore ordered English marines to place cannons around the Governor's Mansion. Then the governor warned that if he was attacked, he would shell Williamsburg and burn it to the ground.

As Henry's militia troops neared the capital, people cheered. The troops stopped 15 miles (24 km) from town. Henry sent a messenger demanding payment for the gunpowder. Frightened officials agreed to pay. Henry's small army backed down. But on May 6, Dunsmore printed a poster. It declared that Patrick Henry was an outlaw. People were ordered to have nothing to do with the outlaw. The effect of Dunsmore's poster, however, was to make Henry a local hero.

Commander Henry

THE SECOND Continental Congress met in 1775. George Washington was named as commander-in-chief of the Colonial Army in Boston. But most delegates still wanted peace with England. Only a few called for total American independence.

Back in Virginia, Henry was picked to lead the Virginia Patriots' force. He had no military training, but when people heard he was commander, enlistment rose sharply. By October 1775, Commander Henry led a force of 1,000 troops. There were so few weapons the men were told to use their squirrel guns. Meanwhile, Lord Dunsmore had left Williamsburg on a British naval ship.

Henry wasn't much of a general. He wasn't very strict and had no military experience. In early 1776, he resigned his commission.

Actors play a scene in which Patrick Henry, right, talks with a military commander in St. John's Church in Richmond, Virginia.

Governor of Virginia

ON JULY 4, 1776, the Second Continental Congress approved the Declaration of Independence in Philadelphia. The declaration was written by Thomas Jefferson. It said that America was free from British rule. Patrick Henry was not there. He was back in Virginia adopting a new state government.

Henry had been elected governor of Virginia on June 29, 1776. In those days, Virginia included the modern states of Kentucky and West Virginia, along with parts of Maryland, Pennsylvania, Ohio, Indiana, and Illinois. When Governor Henry began his job, the western regions were under heavy Indian attack. To the east, Henry had to arm ships to fight the British navy. He also needed to recruit soldiers for Washington's Continental Army.

Facing page: an actor portraying Patrick Henry, governor of Virginia.

The War Years

IN HENRY'S SECOND one-year term as governor, on October 9, 1777, he married Dorothea Dandridge. Dandridge was 20 years younger than Henry. Dorothea's grandfather was once the colonial governor of Virginia, and she was a cousin of George Washington's wife, Martha.

The war went badly for the Continental Army. Washington lost many battles. Many people said that the general should be fired, but Henry stayed loyal to Washington. In the winter of 1777-78, Washington's troops were freezing and starving to death at Valley Forge, Pennsylvania. Henry worked frantically to get food and clothing to the soldiers.

After three terms as governor, Henry was limited by law from running again for at least four years. Thomas Jefferson succeeded him as governor. Around that time, British forces were closing in on Virginia. There were not enough

Continental soldiers in the state to stop them. British troops soon captured Richmond, Portsmouth, and other key areas. One British raiding party set out to arrest Henry and Jefferson. The Americans barely escaped capture.

In 1780, Henry was elected to the Virginia House. In 1783, Washington defeated the British troops in Yorktown, Virginia. The war was over. America was free. In 1784, Henry was elected governor of Virginia once again.

Rembrandt Peale's painting of General George Washington before the Battle of Yorktown.

Constitutional Convention

AMERICANS CELEBRATED the end of the Revolutionary War, but there were problems with the new government. The states did not want to pay taxes to a central government. And states had bitter trade disputes between them.

In 1787, a meeting was called to write a plan for a new government. It was called the Constitutional Convention. Henry was elected to the Constitutional Convention, but refused to serve.

After a long, hot summer in Philadelphia, the new Constitution was written. Each state then had to ratify (approve) it. When it came time for Virginia to ratify, Patrick Henry was dead set against the Constitution.

Henry fought against the Constitution for three weeks. He argued against a strong central government. He thought that the fast-growing

Independence Hall, in Philadelphia, Pennsylvania, site of the Constitutional Convention of 1787.

northern states would have too much power over the farming states in the South.

Henry had helped write Virginia's Constitution. It guaranteed freedom of speech, religion, and other liberties. He refused to support a Constitution that did not have a bill of rights to protect these freedoms. Henry called the United States Constitution "the most fatal plan that could possibly be conceived to enslave a free people."

Other delegates at the Constitutional Convention argued in favor of the Constitution. They pointed out that George Washington would be the first president. This swayed the argument in their favor. The delegates trusted Washington, who was a war hero and a Virginian.

The delegates voted 89 to 79 to ratify the United States Constitution. Henry graciously accepted defeat and said he would remain a loyal citizen. Later, his demands were met when the Bill of Rights were added to the Constitution.

The Final Years

ONCE GEORGE WASHINGTON became president, he offered Henry several jobs. Washington asked him to be the American Ambassador to Spain, Secretary of State, or Chief Justice of the Supreme Court. Henry wasn't interested.

Henry continued to work as a lawyer. And he kept buying and selling land—he was one of the 100 largest landholders in Virginia. Henry had a huge family to support. He had six children from his first marriage and 11 children with his second wife.

In 1799, Henry was easily elected to the Virginia House, but he was too ill to ever take office. On June 6, 1799, Patrick Henry died at home. He was 63 years old.

Despite offers by George Washington of top political jobs, Patrick Henry chose to stay in Virginia and continue his work as a lawyer.

Conclusion

PATRICK HENRY'S SLOGAN, "Give me liberty or give me death!" has been an American motto for over two centuries. In times of peace, Henry rallied people with his words. In times of war, he moved people with his actions. After he died, Thomas Jefferson described Henry's fame:

"He was as well suited to the times as any man ever was, and it is not now easy to say what we should have done without Patrick Henry."

Facing page: a portrait of Patrick Henry, political leader and celebrated orator of the American Revolution.

Timeline

May 29, 1736 Patrick Henry born at Studley Plantation in Hanover County, Virginia.

1754 .... Marries Sarah Shelton.

1760 .... Admitted to the bar, starts law practice.

1763 .... Gives famous "Parson's Cause" speech.

1765 .... Elected to Virginia's House of Burgesses. Gives famous "Stamp Act" speech.

1774 .... Elected to represent Virginia at the First Continental Congress in Philadelphia.

1775 .... Henry's wife, Sarah Shelton, dies. Gives famous "Give me Liberty or Give me Death" speech.

1776–1779 .... Governor of Virginia.

1777 .... Marries Dorothea Dandridge.

1780–1784 .... Member of the House of Delegates representing Hanover County.

1784–1786 .... Reelected as Governor of Virginia.

1795 .... Refuses President Washington's request to serve as Secretary of State.

1796 .... Refuses President Washington's request to serve as Chief Justice of the Supreme Court. Refuses offer from the Virginia General Assembly to serve as Governor. Elected to the Virginia House, but never took office.

June 6, 1799 .. Dies at home. Buried at Red Hill, Charlotte County, Virginia.

Where on the Web?

The American Revolution Home Page
http://webpages.homestead.com/revwar/files/
HENRY.HTM

Brian Tubb's If This Be Treason
http://www.suite101.com/article.cfm/
us_founding_era/45545

U.S. History's Declaration of Independence
Related Information - People
http://www.ushistory.org/declaration/related/
henry.htm

The Association for the Preservation of Virginia
Antiquities
http://www.apva.org/apva/phenry.html

The History Explorer of Colonial Williamsburg
http://63.111.53.150/Almanack/people/bios/
biohen.htm

Glossary

American Revolution: the war between Great Britain and its American Colonies that lasted from 1775 to 1783. America won its independence in the war.

boycott: to try to change the actions of a company or government by refusing to buy their products.

The Colonies: the British territories that made up the first 13 states of the United States. The 13 colonies included New Hampshire, Massachusetts, Rhode Island, Connecticut, New York, New Jersey, Pennsylvania, Delaware, Maryland, Virginia, North Carolina, South Carolina, and Georgia.

Constitution: the document that spells out the principles and laws governing the United States.

Constitutional Convention: the meeting of men who wrote the United States Constitution.

Continental Army: the army that fought the British in the Revolutionary War.

Continental Congress: lawmakers who governed the 13 Colonies after they declared their independence from Great Britain.

debate: to discuss an issue in order to reach the best solution.

Declaration of Independence: the document written by Thomas Jefferson that declared America's independence from Great Britain.

effigy: a stuffed dummy meant to symbolize a living person.

Federalist: a political party that favors a strong central government over the states.

House of Representatives: a governing body elected by popular vote to rule a nation.

militia: a group of citizens enrolled in military service during a time of emergency.

Index